Reading
Renaissance
Library

MINI-LESSONS:
A SAMPLER

The Institute for Academic Excellence, Inc.
Madison, Wisconsin

The Accelerated Reader® and Reading Renaissance® are registered trademarks of Advantage Learning Systems, Inc. The Institute for Academic Excellence is a service mark of Advantage Learning Systems, Inc.

The K-W-L Interactive Reading Strategy on page 62 is reprinted by permission of Donna Ogle, Ed.D., National-Louis University, from "K-W-L: A Teaching Model That Develops Active Reading of Expository Text," *The Reading Teacher*, February 1986, pp. 564-570.

The Institute for Academic Excellence, Inc.
P.O. Box 45016
Madison, WI 53744-5016
(800) 200-4848

CONTENTS

MINI-LESSONS AND
READING RENAISSANCE

The goal of all reading instruction is to help students become lifelong learners who love to read. Research tells us that in order for this to happen, students must spend a substantial amount of time reading books. Using the power of learning information systems, Reading Renaissance enables teachers to manage this kind of extensive, literature-based reading practice. As a result, students' reading skills grow. At the same time, students are introduced to the wonderful world of books and develop a love of reading and learning that will serve them well throughout their lifetime.

For many schools, however, the notion of devoting so much time to literature-based reading practice is new, even anxiety provoking. The first question most teachers ask is, "How can I give my students an hour of reading practice every day and still teach the reading skills that I know are needed and that our curriculum requires me to teach?" The answer is mini-lessons. Short and sharply focused, mini-lessons balance reading instruction and reading practice. They can be used to teach nearly every skill, and they accommodate various teaching styles and instructional techniques. Teachers who use mini-lessons find that they are key to teaching students the skills they need to learn and giving students the time they need to transfer and practice those skills.

WHAT ARE MINI-LESSONS?

Mini-lessons are 10- to 15-minute lessons that deal with a single objective and are integrated with the books that students are reading on their own. The format is straightforward. The teacher presents a skill, using examples from books with which students are familiar, often books that she is currently reading aloud to them. Students look for additional examples in their own books. During reading practice time, which follows a mini-lesson, the teacher takes the Status of the Class. As she talks to each of her students individually, she checks to see if they have understood the mini-lesson and helps them apply the skill to their own reading.

Mini-lessons are not, of course, a new concept. Many teachers have discovered that 15 minutes is about how long most students can focus on one idea or activity. Mini-lessons are, however, especially relevant to Reading Renaissance. As stream-lined bursts of instruction, they free up time for the accountable reading practice that is the heart of Reading Renaissance. And as a literature-based instructional format, they keep our ultimate goal front and center: to help students perfect their skills so that they can more easily read for pleasure and to learn.

MINI-LESSONS AND THE READING RENAISSANCE WORKSHOP

Mini-lessons are an important component of what we call the Reading Renaissance Workshop. This is the part of the school day that combines instruction with reading practice and one-on-one contact with students. For a class of established readers, we suggest devoting about 75 minutes a day to the Reading Renaissance Workshop. For emergent readers, we suggest about two hours daily. The basic components of the Reading Renaissance Workshop are:

Mini-Lessons. The short skill lesson you teach often will include reading to students and discussing a familiar book to give specific examples from literature of the skill you are teaching.

Reading Practice Time. For established readers, this is time that students spend reading independently. We recommend 60 minutes daily. For emergent readers, reading time includes more Read To and Read With time, with as much time for independent reading as students can handle. (The chart on the next page lists specific grade-level recommendations.) To achieve optimal reading growth, students should read within their Zone of Proximal Development (ZPD)—the range of book readability levels that will challenge but not frustrate them.

RECOMMENDED AVERAGE MINUTES OF READING PRACTICE TIME

Grade	Read To	Read With	Read Independently
K - 1st semester	30	0	0
K - 2nd semester	30	5	5
1 - 1st semester	30	10	10
1 - 2nd semester	15	15	30
2 - 1st semester	15	10	35
2 - 2nd semester	15	5	40
3 and up	5 - 15	5 - 15	60

Accelerated Reader® Quizzes. After students complete books, they take AR quizzes. Quizzes motivate students to read and help you guide and monitor your students' reading progress. They're quick, too, so that students can get back to reading practice.

Status of the Class. As students read independently, you visit briefly with each of them to check on their application of the skill you've taught, review their Student Reading Log, and talk about the book they are reading.

The Reading Renaissance Workshop will look different depending on whether your class consists primarily of established readers or emergent readers. In classes of established readers (usually grades three and up), you will use the first 10 to 15 minutes for a mini-lesson, and then follow up with 60 minutes of practice time, during which students select books, read, and take AR quizzes, and you take Status of the Class. Read With activities, for students who need them, also take place during this time.

In classes of emergent readers (usually prekindergarten through grade two), you will want to implement the Reading Renaissance workshop gradually. We recommend that you begin with lots of Read To time and book discussions, gradually add more Read

With time, and then move on to Independent Reading time, increasing the amount as students' skills develop. During the workshop, students will take AR quizzes on books that have been Read To and Read With them, as well as books they may have read on their own. The Primary Reading Log will help you keep track of students' reading in class and at home. You also can make good use of mini-lessons at this level, building phonemic awareness, teaching decoding strategies, and developing comprehension skills.

READING RENAISSANCE WORKSHOP COMPONENTS

1. Mini-lessons can include
   • Read To
   • Book discussions

2. Reading practice time—60 minutes includes
   • Status of the Class
   • AR quizzes
   • Read With, as appropriate

WHERE DO IDEAS FOR MINI-LESSONS COME FROM?

You can use the mini-lesson format to teach any kind of reading skill, including word identification skills, vocabulary, comprehension, literary skills, and study skills. Your existing curriculum will fuel the content. So will the needs of your students. By taking the Status of the Class daily, you will have many opportunities to observe how your students are doing and determine which skills they need to learn or practice.

We have included thirty mini-lessons in this book for you to use, as appropriate, with your students. But, of course, they will make up only a handful of the mini-lessons that you will present in the course of a school year. Where will you find ideas for creating the others? In the same places you have found ideas for traditional lessons: basal readers, district or state curriculum guides, professional journals, and workshops. Moreover, you will discover that many of your favorite lessons can easily be transformed into mini-lessons by breaking them into smaller pieces and incorporating the elements listed below.

ELEMENTS OF A MINI-LESSON

The lessons included in this book are intended to be models as well as actual lessons that you can present to students. As you read through them and use them in your classroom, you will notice that they have certain elements in common. These are the elements that you will use when creating your own mini-lessons.

Mini-lessons are short. A good mini-lesson takes only 10 to 15 minutes to present. When a skill is complex or has multiple parts, we suggest presenting a series of mini-lessons on that skill over the course of two or more days. You'll find examples of a skill presented in several mini-lessons on pages 21, 41, 52, and 77. You also may want to review a specific skill throughout the school year with periodic, brief mini-lessons.

Mini-lessons have a clear objective. Since you have only 15 minutes to present a skill, you must keep your objective firmly in mind. You will find that a mini-lesson works best when it has a single objective that is easily stated.

Mini-lessons rely on literature as the vehicle for instruction and practice. When possible, use the book that you are currently reading aloud to students as a source of examples for the skill you are teaching. Ask students to look for examples in the books they are reading independently (or, in the case of younger students, other books that have been read aloud to them or read with them). Immediately follow the mini-lesson with reading practice time, and direct students to look for additional examples or to apply a skill you have just taught as they read on their own. These "assignments," however, should be simple and short so that students can stay focused on the books they are reading. For example, while it would be a good idea to ask students to look for two examples of a compound word as they read, asking them to list all the compound words they find would be distracting.

The impact of a mini-lesson is assessed during Status of the Class. As you talk to each student, ask questions that will help you determine whether the student has understood the lesson. After a lesson on cause and effect, for example, you might ask students, "What happened in the last chapter of your book? Why did it happen? What caused the character to feel this way? What was the effect of this character's actions?"

Skills taught in mini-lessons can be reinforced with other activities. With each mini-lesson in this book, we include suggestions for added practice. You can use these practice activities during the days following the mini-lesson to reinforce the instruction, or you can use them later in the year as part of a mini-lesson that covers the same subject but uses a different book. You also might offer them to a smaller group of students who need more practice in that specific skill. As you create your own mini-lessons, you may want to similarly note activities that students can do for additional practice, as needed.

As you look over the lessons in this book, you'll notice that they employ a variety of teaching strategies, including teacher modeling, K-W-L charts, story maps, and webs. All of these strategies—along with many other instructional techniques—are easily incorporated into the mini-lesson format. Your choice of one over the other will depend on what you have found works best with your students. The important thing to remember about mini-lessons is that while the content and teaching strategy may vary, the basic elements, as outlined above, remain the same.

MINI-LESSONS: A SAMPLER

These thirty lessons are intended to show how the mini-lesson format can be used to teach a wide range of skills. Each mini-lesson has been developed with a particular grade grouping in mind. (See chart on page 7.) You can easily adapt most of them, however, to other levels, and we encourage you to do so. And while we give examples of specific books that we believe are well suited to the lessons, you can use many others with equal success. Most of all, we hope this sampler will inspire you to develop engaging, creative lessons that will help every one of your students discover the joy of reading.

SKILLS COVERED IN THESE MINI-LESSONS

Skill Strand	Primary (K-2)	Intermediate (3-5)	Middle School (6-8)	High School (9-12)
Reading Renaissance Skill	Book Selection	Using ZPD		
Word Identification	CVCe Words Compound Words	Syllabication Prefixes and Suffixes		
Vocabulary	Using Context Clues	Homonyms	Using Context Clues	Words From Greek and Latin
Comprehension	Predicting Outcomes	Elements of a Story Cause and Effect Sequence Characterization Main Idea	Drawing Conclusions Fact and Opinion	Point of View Summarizing
Literary Skills		Genre: Folktales	Figures of Speech Genre: Mystery Genre: Historical Fiction Genre: Biography	Author's Purpose Theme
Study Skills		Dictionary Skills	Note Taking Analogies	

BOOK SELECTION

GRADE LEVEL : Primary (K-2)

OBJECTIVE : To help students select books

MATERIALS : A variety of AR books representing a range of appropriate ZPD levels (each book should be color coded or labeled with its reading level); one or two AR books that have intriguing covers but that are written at a level well above students' abilities

LESSON : **1.** Place a selection of books along the chalk tray or in another location where all students can see them clearly. On the chalkboard, draw a large outline of a book.

2. Ask volunteers to come up one at a time and point to a book he or she might like to read. After a volunteer makes a choice, ask: "Which book did you choose? Why do you think you might like that book?"

3. Record students' responses to the second question inside the outline of the book. Possible responses include:
- ◆ I liked the picture on the cover.
- ◆ Someone told me about the book.
- ◆ I've read this book before and I liked it.
- ◆ The book is about dinosaurs, and I like dinosaurs.
- ◆ I always like books written by this author.

4. Tell students that their methods for choosing certain books are good ones and that all readers use them at one time or another. Then hold up one of the difficult books. Say, "I thought I'd like this book because I like horses and there is a horse on the cover. When I tried to read the book, however, I discovered that it's way too hard for me. What clues might have told me it was too hard?" Students suggestions may include:
- ◆ There weren't any pictures inside.
- ◆ The type was small.
- ◆ It was a thick book with a lot of pages.

5. Next, select a book with a ZPD level appropriate for most students. Point to the color code or reading-level label on the book, and explain that it will help them find books that are not too hard (and, for older students, not too easy).

6. In a special corner of the chalkboard, list the color(s) and level(s) appropriate for most students. Tell students that knowing these codes will help them choose books that they will understand and enjoy.

STATUS OF THE CLASS FOLLOW-UP

As you take the Status of the Class, ask:
  ◆ Why did you choose this book?
  ◆ Which parts of the book did you look at while you were making your choice?
  ◆ What is the color code or label on this book?
  ◆ Does the book seem too hard or too easy for you?
  ◆ Do you think that the next time you choose a book, you'd like to try one that is harder or easier?

If necessary, adjust students' book ranges to fit their ZPD levels and introduce them to the new color code or label.

ADDED PRACTICE

  ◆ Students can make jackets for books they would like to recommend to classmates. Suggest that students draw an illustration and write the book's title and author on the front cover. On the back cover, help them write one or two sentences telling why they liked the book. Have students include the book's color code or reading level in an appropriate place on the book jacket. Post the jackets on a bulletin board near the classroom library.

  ◆ Briefly discuss how books are sorted in your school or classroom library. Give pairs of students a pile of books to sort. Have each pair work together to sort the books in as many different ways as possible—by topic, by author, by length, by number of illustrations, by color code, and so on. Create a list of the different ways books can be sorted and discuss the advantages and disadvantages of each.

CVCe Words

GRADE LEVEL   Primary (K-2)

OBJECTIVE   To help students decode words that have a consonant-vowel-consonant-*e* spelling pattern

MATERIALS   Any book that you are currently reading to students, such as *Frog and Toad Are Friends* by Arnold Lobel (1.4); large index cards or strips of tagboard; marker

LESSON   **1.** On the left side of the index card or tagboard strip, print a word that can be changed by adding a silent *e* to the end, such as *cap, not*, or *hat*. Fold over a flap on the right side of the card and print the letter *e* on the back of the flap as shown.

2. Tell students that you are going to perform a magic trick. Show students the card with the flap unfolded and ask them to read the word *hat* aloud. Then fold the flap over and help them read the new word, *hate*. Ask, "What is the sound of the letter *a* in this word?" (\\ā\\ or long a)

3. Repeat the procedure for the words *cap* and *cape*. Then explain, "When a word ends with a vowel-consonant-*e*, the *e* is silent. The silent *e* gives the vowel a long sound."

4. Read a passage from your current Read To book, and pause to point out one or two CVCe words. In *Frog and Toad Are Friends*, for example, the word *wake* appears on the first page. Write the word on the board. Ask, "Which letter is silent? What sound does the silent *e* give the *a*?" Ask students to look in their books for examples of CVCe words. Repeat these questions with words that they find.

5. Ask students to see if they can find two more silent *e* words as they read their books. You also may want to pause briefly to point out CVCe words as you read aloud during Read To time.

STATUS OF THE CLASS FOLLOW-UP

As you take the Status of the Class, ask:

◆ Have you found any silent *e* words in your book? Can you read each word?

◆ How does knowing about the silent *e* help you read the word?

If a student stumbles while reading a CVCe word, point to the *e* and say, "This word has a silent *e*. What sound does the silent *e* give the other vowel?" Gradually, simply pointing to the *e* will be a strong enough cue for decoding the word.

ADDED PRACTICE

◆ Students can make word slides out of two strips of tagboard. Help them cut two slits in one strip and print an *e* after the slits as shown. On a longer strip, have them write a list of rhyming CVC words and nonsense syllables, such as *cat, dat, fat, gat, hat, lat,* and so on. Show students how to slip the longer strip into the slits of the shorter strip and pull it through to see how many words they can make with a silent *e*.

mat
gat
fat

hat e

◆ Encourage students to make up stories about the magical or heroic "E" following this pattern:

Once there was a sad old man sitting by the side of the road with nothing but an old tin can. Magical "E" came by and said, "Old man, why are you so sad?"

"My foot hurts, and I've lost my cane," cried the old man.

"Oh, I can take care of that!" exclaimed "E." She touched the can, and—PRESTO!—it was a cane!

COMPOUND WORDS

GRADE LEVEL : Primary (K-2)

OBJECTIVE : To help students decode compound words by breaking them into smaller words

MATERIALS : Any book you are currently reading to students, such as *Nate the Great and the Musical Note* by Marjorie and Craig Sharmat (1.6); tagboard; marker; scissors

LESSON : **1.** Write the word *doghouse* on a strip of tagboard. Read the word aloud. Then cut the strip so that the words *dog* and *house* are on separate halves. Ask volunteers to read each smaller word.

2. Tell students that a word made from two small words put together is called a *compound word*. Breaking compound words into smaller words can help readers pronounce the longer word and figure out what it means.

3. Read a passage from your current Read To book and pause to point out compound words. In *Nate the Great and the Musical Note*, for example, the words *bathtub* and *doorbell* appear on the first page. Write the words on tagboard strips and ask volunteers to cut each longer word apart to make two smaller words. Have students read aloud the smaller words and the compound word they make when they are put together.

4. Ask students to see if they can find two compound words as they read their books. You also may want to pause briefly to point out compound words as you read aloud during Read To time.

STATUS OF THE CLASS FOLLOW-UP

As you take the Status of the Class, ask:
- ◆ Have you found any compound words in your book?
- ◆ What are the smaller words that make up the long word?
- ◆ Does knowing the two smaller words help you figure out the longer word?

If a compound word causes a student to stumble while reading aloud, show the student how covering one of the smaller words with a finger and reading the smaller words separately will help him pronounce the word and figure out what it means.

ADDED PRACTICE

- ◆ Help students write compound words that they find in their books on index cards. Separate each compound word into its smaller words by cutting it into two puzzle pieces. Have students put the puzzle pieces together to form and read compound words.

- ◆ Help students brainstorm compound words that contain the same smaller word, such as *ball* or *day*. List the words and talk about their meanings.

foot<u>ball</u>	<u>day</u>time
base<u>ball</u>	<u>day</u>dream
<u>ball</u>park	Sun<u>day</u>

Using Context Clues

GRADE LEVEL : Primary (K-2)

OBJECTIVE : To help students use context clues to figure out unfamiliar words

MATERIALS : Any book you are currently reading to students, such as *George and Martha* by James Marshall (2.5)

LESSON : **1.** Write a sentence on the chalkboard that contains an unfamiliar word, for example, "How do you expect to walk home with your *loafers* full of split pea soup?" from *George and Martha*. Ask, "When you are reading and you come across a word you don't understand or can't pronounce, what can you do to figure it out?"

2. Discuss students' suggestions. Possible responses include:
   ◆ Ask the teacher or another student.
   ◆ Try to sound it out.

Then tell students they also can figure out a word they don't know by looking at the other words and sentences around the word. Reread the sentence and ask, "What word or words in this sentence might give you a clue that would help you figure out the word *loafers*?" (walk)

3. Tell students that when they are reading by themselves they can use clues to figure out words they don't know. Write a different sentence on the board, replacing one word with a blank, for example, "From now on, you'll never have to eat that _____ soup again." Read the sentence aloud and ask students to predict what the word is by using clues in the sentence. List predictions on the board, adding a few of your own, including *awful*.

4. Now add an *a* and an *l* at the beginning and end of the blank in the sentence, so that it looks like this: a_____l. Ask, "Look at the letters at the beginning and end of the missing word. What are some words that begin and end with these letter sounds? List students' suggestions on the board. (animal, April, apple, awful)

5. Reread the sentence. Compare the two lists of words and ask, "Is there a word in these lists that both makes sense in this sentence and has the same beginning and ending letter sounds?" (yes, *awful*)

6. Conclude by saying, "When you come to a word you don't know while you are reading, stop and think about the other words in the sentence. They might give you clues that will help you figure out the word."

STATUS OF THE CLASS FOLLOW-UP

As you take the Status of the Class, ask:
- Have you come across a word you don't know while you've been reading?
- What have you done to figure out the word?
- What else could you have done if you still didn't know the word?

If while reading aloud a student gets stuck when she comes to a new word, have her skip the word and read on. Then encourage her to go back and try to use context clues to figure out the word.

ADDED PRACTICE

- On the chalkboard or individual sheets of paper, write a brief paragraph about the day's activities or copy a passage from a familiar book. Erase or cross out every fifth or sixth word. Then challenge students to use context clues to figure out what the missing words are.

- Suggest that pairs of students play "Pickle." Partners take turns making up sentences with strong context clues and replacing a key word with the word *pickle,* for example, "My pet PICKLE loves to chase mice." Partners try to predict each other's mystery words.

PREDICTING OUTCOMES

GRADE LEVEL : Primary (K-2)

OBJECTIVE : To help students develop strategies for predicting outcomes

MATERIALS : *Ira Sleeps Over* by Bernard Waber (2.8); a large, heavy book

LESSON : **1.** Place a large book precariously on the edge of a desk or table. Pretend you are about to bump the book with your hand or elbow. Just before you do, ask, "What do you think will happen next?" After students have given their suggestions, proceed to knock the book off the table. Ask, "How did you know that was going to happen?"

2. Point out that students used both what they saw (that you were about to bump the book) and what they already knew (that things pushed too far over the edge of a table fall on the floor) to figure out what they thought would happen next. Explain that they can use the same information to predict what will happen next in a story.

3. Begin reading aloud *Ira Sleeps Over*. Stop before Ira goes to Reggie's house for the sleepover. Ask, "What do you think will happen next. Will Ira take his teddy bear to Reggie's house?"

4. Draw two large circles on the chalkboard. Label the circles, "What We Know From the Story" and "What We Know From Real Life." Below the circles, draw another circle labeled "What We Think Will Happen." Write the students' prediction in that circle. (If opinions are sharply divided, you may want to create one diagram for each prediction.)

5. Ask students to help you fill in the other two circles by asking questions, such as:
- ◆ What in the story makes you think Ira will (or won't) take his teddy?
- ◆ If you were Ira, would you take your teddy? Why or why not?

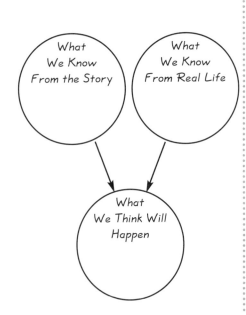

◆ Have you ever been in a situation like this one? What did you do?

6. Finish reading the story. Ask, "Did Ira do what you thought he would do?"

7. Tell students that thinking about what will happen next in stories they read will help them better understand the stories and enjoy them more. Remind students to think about what is happening in the story as well as what they know from their own lives as they try to figure out what will happen next.

STATUS OF THE CLASS FOLLOW-UP

As you take the Status of the Class, ask:
◆ What is happening in the story right now?
◆ Has anything like this ever happened to you or to someone you know?
◆ What do you think will happen next? Why?

ADDED PRACTICE

◆ Have students fold sheets of drawing paper in half. On one half of the paper, ask students to draw a picture of what they think will happen next in the story they are reading. After students finish reading their stories, have them draw a picture of what actually happened next in the story.

◆ Older students can divide sheets of notebook paper into three columns and label the columns "What I Think Will Happen," "Why I Think It Will Happen," and "What Happened." As students read, have them write down what they think will happen, their reasons for their predictions, and what actually happened in the story.

USING ZPD

GRADE LEVEL : Intermediate (3-5)

OBJECTIVE : To help students use their ZPD to select books

MATERIALS : A variety of AR books about animals that together represent a wide range of reading levels (each book should be labeled with its reading level and AR point value); student reading log

LESSON : **1.** Display the books and ask, "Suppose you wanted to read a story about animals. How would you go about finding a book that is just right for you?"

2. Discuss students' responses. Possible responses include:
  ◆ Look at the cover.
  ◆ See how big the print is.
  ◆ Look at the pictures inside.
  ◆ Read a little bit of it.

3. Tell students that sometimes it's difficult to know if a book is too easy or too hard just by looking at it. Then point to the reading label on one of the books and say, "These labels can help you figure out how hard or easy a book will be to read." Explain that knowing how to use the reading-level labels on AR books will help them choose books that are just right for them.

4. Talk with students briefly about the best way to practice a skill—catching a ball, for example. Point out that if, during practice time, someone always threw balls directly to them, the balls would be so easy to catch that they would never learn how to catch balls that were thrown a little high or a little far away. At the same time, if someone always threw balls so high or so far away that they could not catch any of them, they would become frustrated and maybe even give up trying. Help students understand that the best way to improve a skill is with practice that is neither too hard nor too easy.

5. Write the letters ZPD on the chalkboard. Tell students that the letters stand for "zone of proximal development," a scientific name for an idea that can help students find the level at which they will get the most from reading practice. Remind students that just as people grow at different rates, their reading abilities grow at different rates. Stress that for this reason, each reader has her own ZPD level. Point out also that as each person's reading ability improves, she moves into a new ZPD.

6. Ask, "If you read a lot of books that were way too easy for you, how would you probably feel?" (bored, uninterested) "On the other hand, if you read a lot of books that were way too hard, how would you feel?" (frustrated, uninterested) Tell students that their individual ZPD will help them find books that are neither too hard nor too easy, but just right for them. Write the following on the chalkboard and say, "Here's a motto for ZPD":

> *Reading books that are too easy can make your brain flabby.*
> *Reading books that are too hard can make your brain crabby.*
> *Keep your brain healthy; read in your ZPD.*

7. Show a sample reading log, and point out where the ZPD is written on the log. Compare the sample ZPD to the reading-level label on a number of books and ask, "Would this be a good book for this student to read?"

8. Remind students that knowing their ZPDs and checking them against book labels will help them choose books that are challenging but not too hard. Then ask, "What if you have been reading and taking quizzes and think that you're ready for some different kinds of books, that maybe what you are reading is too easy?" Students may come up with the idea that their reading ability has improved and that they need to read in a higher ZPD. Confirm their suspicions by telling them that will indeed happen as they read more and more. Remind them that their ZPD is only a guide and that though they might keep their eye on their ZPD, they should also follow their interests, favorite authors, and others' recommendations when choosing books to read. By reading books that both interest them and are within their ZPD, they will continue to grow as readers.

Continued on next page

STATUS OF THE CLASS FOLLOW-UP

As you take the Status of the Class, ask:

◆ What attracted you to this book?

◆ How did knowing your ZPD help you choose this book?

◆ Do you feel that you will do well on the AR quiz for this book? Why or why not?

◆ Is your ZPD always going to be the same as it is today? When will it change?

◆ Do you think we need to adjust your ZPD now? Why?

ADDED PRACTICE

◆ Students can make bookmarks on which they write their name and current ZPD. Suggest that students carry their bookmarks with them as they choose books to read.

◆ AR software can create customized book lists for each student based on her current ZPD level and other criteria. This may be a good time to give each student her customized list.

◆ Groups of students reading within the same ZPD can make posters listing their favorite books in that zone. Mount the posters near the classroom library so that they can serve as quick references for others.

PREFIXES AND SUFFIXES

GRADE LEVEL : Intermediate (3-5)

OBJECTIVE : To help students decode words and figure out their meanings by recognizing prefixes and suffixes

MATERIALS : A shoe with shoelaces untied

LESSON : You may wish to teach prefixes and suffixes over the course of two days.

Day One : **1.** Hold up the untied shoe and ask, "What can I do with these shoelaces?" As students answer, tie the laces and write the word *tie* on the chalkboard.

2. Tell students that a root word is a word to which other word parts can be added to make new words. Point to the word *tie* and say, "*Tie* is a root word."

3. Ask, "Suppose I want to put this shoe on. Now what must I do?" Untie the laces and write *untie* on the chalkboard. Ask, "If I want to tie these laces together again, what must I do?" Retie the laces and write *retie* on the board.

4. Circle the word part *un-* in *untie*. Explain that *un-* is a prefix or word part that is added to the beginning of a root word to make a new word. Ask, "If *un-* means 'not,' then what does the word *untie* mean?" Repeat the procedure with *retie,* asking, "If *re-* means 'again,' what does the word *retie* mean?"

5. List a few prefixes and their meanings on the chalkboard. Ask students to look through their books for words that contain these prefixes. As you write each example on the board, help students identify the root word and prefix. Then have students use the meanings of the root word and prefix to figure out the meaning of the larger word.

6. Ask students to see if they can find two words that contain prefixes as they read their books. Tell them that knowing how to break words into prefixes and root words will help them figure out the meaning of new words they come across.

Day Two

1. On the chalkboard, draw the outline of a tree with four or five large branches. Remind students that a root word is a word to which other word parts can be added to make new words and that a prefix can be added to the beginning of a root word to make a new word.

2. Write the root word *help* on the trunk of the tree. On one of the branches, write the word *helpful*. Circle *-ful* and say, "Word parts like this one are added to the end of root words to make new words. These word parts are called suffixes." Ask students to list other words that contain the root word *help* and a suffix, for example, *helper, helping, helpless, helped*. Write each word on a branch of the tree.

3. Erase the words in the tree and write the word *dance* on the trunk. On the branches, write *danced, dancing, dancer*. Ask, "What happened to the spelling of the root word when the suffixes were added?" Follow the same procedure for the root words *funny (funnier, funniest)* and *swim (swimmer, swimming)*. Explain that even though the spelling of the root word might change when a suffix is added, the meanings of the root word and the suffix do not change.

4. Erase the words in the tree again, and ask students to look in their books for words that contain suffixes. Ask a volunteer to write a word with a suffix on a branch of the tree and its root word on the tree trunk. Then ask the class to help fill in branches with other words containing the root word and a prefix or suffix. Tell students that knowing how to break words into suffixes and root words will help them pronounce new words they come across as they read.

STATUS OF THE CLASS FOLLOW-UP

As you take the Status of the Class, ask:
- ◆ Have you found any words that contain prefixes or suffixes?
- ◆ Does the word have a prefix or a suffix?
- ◆ What is the meaning of the root word? What is the meaning of the prefix (or suffix)?
- ◆ How does breaking the word into the root word and the prefix or suffix help you pronounce the word and figure out its meaning? If a student stumbles over a word with a prefix or suffix while reading, show him how to frame the root word with his fingers and read the root word first.

ADDED PRACTICE

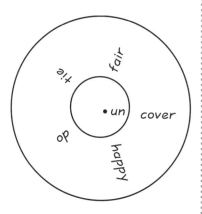

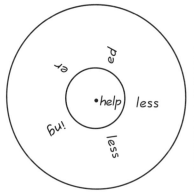

- ◆ Help students make word wheels for prefixes, suffixes, and root words they come across as they read. Cut two circles out of tagboard, one significantly smaller than the other, and use a brass fastener to fasten the two circles together in the center. Print the prefix on the smaller circle and root words on the larger circle. Or, you can write a root word on the smaller circle and suffixes on the larger circle. Students create new words as they turn the circles.

- ◆ Pairs of students can write word equations for each other to solve. Each solution should contain one or more prefix or suffix. Suggest that partners work together to figure out the meanings of the new words they have created.

  re + build = _____
  dis + continue - e + ous = ____

SYLLABICATION

GRADE LEVEL   Intermediate (3-5)

OBJECTIVE   To help students decode words by dividing them into syllables

MATERIALS   Any book you are currently reading to students, such as *From the Mixed-up Files of Mrs. Basil E. Frankweiler* by E. L. Konigsburg (4.8)

LESSON   **1.** On the chalkboard, list words that reflect the three syllabication rules given below in step 3. You may wish to use words from your current Read To book, such as these, which appear in *From the Mixed-up Files of Mrs. Basil E. Frankweiler:*

> mummy
> Roman
> magic
> marble

2. Remind students that a syllable is a word part that contains one vowel sound. Say a variety of one-, two-, and three-syllable words and ask students how many syllables they hear in each word. Repeat each word, emphasizing the vowel sounds to help students understand that the number of syllables the word has is the same as the number of vowel sounds they hear. Tell students that knowing how to divide words into syllables can help them figure out unknown words.

3. Tell students that there are rules that can help them divide words into syllables. As you explain each of the following rules, draw lines between the syllables in the words on the board.
   - When two consonants come between two vowels, divide the word between the two consonants. (mum / my)
   - When one consonant comes between two vowels, try dividing the word before the consonant and giving the vowel a long vowel sound. (Ro / man) If that doesn't work, divide the word after the consonant and give the vowel a short sound. (mag / ic)

♦ When a word ends with a consonant and *le,* divide the word before the consonant. (mar / ble)

4. Ask students to look through their books for two-syllable words that they think might follow one of the rules you've discussed. Have volunteers write the words on the chalkboard and draw lines to divide their words into syllables. Help students read each syllable aloud and then combine the syllables to read the entire word.

STATUS OF THE CLASS FOLLOW-UP

As you take the Status of the Class, point out a word that follows one of the syllabication rules listed above. Ask:
♦ How would you divide this word into syllables?
♦ Can you read the first syllable? How about the second syllable?
♦ Now put the syllables together again. Can you read the whole word?

ADDED PRACTICE

♦ Write the syllables of familiar words in a scrambled order, as shown below. Have students place the syllables in order and write each word. If you are working with an individual student, write the syllables on note cards. Then have the student place the cards in order and read the word aloud.

| tant | por | im | | important |
| su | he | ro | per | superhero |

♦ Suggest that students keep a running list of interesting words from their books. Have them list their words on sheets of notebook paper divided into four columns labeled *One Syllable, Two Syllables, Three Syllables,* and *Four or More Syllables.* For additional practice, pairs of students can exchange lists and divide words from one anothers' lists into syllables.

HOMONYMS

GRADE LEVEL : Intermediate (3-5)

OBJECTIVE : To help students recognize homonyms and use context clues to determine their meanings

MATERIALS : *Amelia Bedelia* by Peggy Parish (3.1) or another book in the Amelia Bedelia series

LESSON : **1.** Read aloud *Amelia Bedelia.* On the chalkboard, write one of the instructions that Amelia Bedelia misunderstood, for example, *Draw the drapes when the sun comes in.* Ask, "What did Amelia Bedelia think she was supposed to do?" (Draw a picture of the drapes.) Then ask, "What did Mrs. Rogers want her to do?" (Close the drapes.)

2. Circle the word *draw* in the sentence. Point out that the word draw has at least two meanings: to pull closed and to make a picture. Explain that words that sound alike but have different meanings are called *homonyms.* Say, "When you run into a word that has more than one meaning, read the rest of the sentence to see if the other words can help you figure out which meaning makes sense." Then ask, "What other words in the sentence might have helped Amelia Bedelia figure out which meaning made sense?"

3. Ask students if they can think of other homonyms from *Amelia Bedelia* or the books they are reading. List the homonyms on the board, and have volunteers use each one in a sentence.

4. Ask students to see if they can find two more homonyms as they read their books. You also may want to pause briefly to point out homonyms as you read aloud during Read To time.

STATUS OF THE CLASS FOLLOW-UP

As you take the Status of the Class, ask:

◆ Have you found any homonyms in your book?

◆ Which meaning of the word makes sense in this sentence? What other words in the sentence helped you figure out the homonym's meaning?

◆ What could you do if there were no clues in the sentence to help you figure out the meaning of the homonym? (Look up the word in the dictionary. Continue reading and come back to the word later.)

ADDED PRACTICE

◆ Create a master homonym list. Divide a large sheet of butcher paper into alphabetical sections. Encourage students to record on the list any homonyms they come across in their books, along with the other words in the homonym set. You even may wish to set up a friendly competition between groups of students or classes to see whose list is longest at the end of a certain amount of time.

◆ Suggest that students play Homonym Pictionary. To play, pairs of students create lists of ten to twenty homonym pairs. One partner chooses a homonym pair from the list and draws pictures to represent the two meanings, for example, a sail on a sailboat and a yard sale. If the other partner guesses the homonyms, she draws the next set of pictures.

ELEMENTS OF A STORY

GRADE LEVEL : Intermediate (3-5)

OBJECTIVE : To help students identify the basic elements of a story: character, setting, and plot

MATERIALS : Any book you are currently reading to students, such as *M.C. Higgins, the Great* by Virginia Hamilton (5.7)

LESSON :

1. On the chalkboard, draw a large hand and label the thumb and fingers as follows: WHO? WHEN? WHERE? WHAT? WHY OR HOW?

2. Tell students that all stories contain certain elements and that three of these elements are *character, setting,* and *plot.* Explain that one way of finding these elements in a story is to ask yourself the following questions: *Who* is the story about? *When* is the story happening? *Where* is it happening? *What* is the problem in the story? *Why* is there a problem or *how* has the problem been solved? Together, the answers to these questions will give you the story's characters (who), setting (when and where), and plot (what, why, and how).

3. Use a familiar fairy tale, such as "Goldilocks and the Three Bears," to illustrate the elements of a story on the hand diagram. If necessary, have a volunteer give a recap of the story, and then ask, "Who is this story about?" Your completed diagram will look something like the one on this page.

4. Ask students to help you create a hand diagram for your current Read To book. Continue to add information to the diagram as you read the book aloud.

5. Remind students that answering the questions *who, when, where, what, why* and *how* will help them remember the important parts or story elements of their own books.

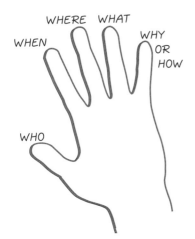

WHO: Goldilocks, the Three Bears
WHEN: Once upon a time
WHERE: The Three Bears' House
WHAT: Goldilocks misuses the Bears' possessions.
WHY OR
    HOW: The Bears come home and scare her

STATUS OF THE CLASS FOLLOW-UP

As you take the Status of the Class, suggest that students hold up a thumb or finger each time you ask:

- ◆ Who is this story about?
- ◆ Where does the story take place?
- ◆ When does the story take place?
- ◆ What is the problem in the story?
- ◆ Why is there a problem? How has the problem been solved?

ADDED PRACTICE

- ◆ Students can trace and cut out their own handprints for books they have read. Suggest that they write the title of the book on the palm of the hand and WHO? WHEN? WHAT? WHERE? and WHY OR HOW?, with the appropriate information about the book, on the fingers and thumb. You may wish to display the completed handprints on a bulletin board.

CAUSE AND EFFECT

GRADE LEVEL : Intermediate (3-5)

OBJECTIVE : To help students identify cause and effect relationships

MATERIALS : Any book you are currently reading to students, such as *Ramona Forever* by Beverly Cleary (4.1); baking soda, vinegar, shallow dish

LESSON : **1.** Place a mound of baking soda in a shallow dish. Hold the dish in plain view of the students. Pour a bit of vinegar over the baking soda. Ask, "What happened?" (The solution began to bubble.) "Why did that happen?" (The vinegar hit the baking soda.)

2. Point out that in this experiment the *cause* of the bubbling was the vinegar hitting the baking soda and the *effect* was the bubbling. Tell students that "why something happened" is called the *cause* and "what happened" is called the *effect*. Explain that cause and effect relationships are found in everyday life, as well as in the stories they read.

3. Introduce students to the idea of cause and effect in stories by asking a few questions about familiar stories, including your current Read To book, such as:
- Why did the Little Red Hen have to bake the bread all by herself? (because no one would help her)
- Why did Robin Hood steal from the rich? (because people were poor and hungry)
- Why didn't Ramona like Uncle Hobart? (because he teased her)

4. For each example, ask students, "What happened?" Then ask, "Why did that happen?" Remind them that the answer to the question "What happened?" is the *effect* and the answer to the question "Why did it happen?" is the *cause*. Point out that in stories, as in real life, we often see the effect of something before we think about or look for the cause.

5. Tell students that sometimes one cause has lots of effects. Write on the chalkboard, "It snowed," and ask students to suggest possible effects. Then explain that many causes also can lead to one effect. Write on the board, "Field day has been canceled," and ask students to suggest a number of possible causes.

6. Ask students to look for cause and effect relationships as they read their books. Remind them to ask themselves "What happened?" to find the effect of an event and "Why did it happen?" to find the cause.

STATUS OF THE CLASS FOLLOW-UP

As you take the Status of the Class, ask:
   ◆ What happened in the last chapter?
   ◆ Why did it happen?
   ◆ What caused this character to feel this way?
   ◆ What was the effect of this character's actions?

ADDED PRACTICE

   ◆ Have students divide a sheet of notebook paper into two columns and label the columns "Cause" and "Effect." As they read their books, have them identify and write a cause on one side of the paper and its effect or effects on the other side. Remind students that in many cases it will be easier to first identify the effect, and then determine the cause or causes.

   ◆ Suggest that students choose a photo from a newspaper or magazine and write a sentence or two explaining either the cause or the effect of the action they see in the photo.

SEQUENCE

GRADE LEVEL : Intermediate (3-5)

OBJECTIVE : To help students identify the order in which things happen in text

MATERIALS : Any book with a straightforward sequence of events, such as *A River Ran Wild* by Lynne Cherry (4.7); large strips of tagboard; masking tape

LESSON : **1.** Read aloud *A River Ran Wild* or another appropriate book. As you read, write the major events on strips of tagboard. For example, events from *A River Ran Wild* might include:

- ◆ Native people settle on the river.
- ◆ European settlers build villages and mills.
- ◆ Native people are driven from the land.
- ◆ Factories dump pollutants into the river.
- ◆ Wildlife dies from the poisons.
- ◆ Oweana and Marion decide to help the river.
- ◆ People start a clean-up campaign.
- ◆ Wildlife returns to the river.

2. On the board, draw a large timeline, story map, or other sequencing graphic. (A river would work well for *A River Ran Wild.*) Be sure that the graphic is divided into as many sections as there are event strips.

3. Shuffle the tagboard strips and place them along the chalk tray. Ask, "Which event happened first?" Ask a volunteer to tape the appropriate card in the proper section on the graphic. Follow the same procedure for the rest of the events.

4. Ask students to keep the sequence of events in mind as they read their books. Remind them that certain clue words, such as *first, next, then,* and *last,* and phrases referring to time (*last Saturday, that night*) tell when things happen. Also warn students that authors do not always use clue words, and they must ultimately rely on their own ideas about which order makes sense.

STATUS OF THE CLASS FOLLOW-UP

As you take the Status of the Class, ask:

- ◆ Can you tell me three (or more) events that have happened in your book so far?
- ◆ In what order did they happen?
- ◆ Did any clue words help you figure out the order? Which words?

ADDED PRACTICE

- ◆ Students can draw comic strips showing a sequence of events from a book they have read. Pairs of students who have read the same book can make comic strips, cut apart the individual frames, and challenge each other to put the strips back in order.

- ◆ Encourage students to create sets of directions for simple tasks, such as brushing teeth, making a peanut-butter sandwich, or looking up a word in the dictionary. Have them include a mistake in each set of directions: a step could be missing, the sequence might be incorrect, or the list might include irrelevant information. Have students exchange lists, correct the sequence, and rewrite the directions in the proper order.

CHARACTERIZATION

GRADE LEVEL : Intermediate (3-5)

OBJECTIVE : To help students identify methods of characterization used by authors

MATERIALS : *The True Story of the Three Little Pigs* by Jon Scieszka (2.2); a standard version of "The Three Little Pigs," such as *The Three Little Pigs and the Big Bad Wolf* by Glen Rounds (3.5) or *The Three Little Pigs: An Old Story* by Margot Zemach (3.5)

LESSON : **1.** On the chalkboard, draw a simple outline of a wolf's head, as shown.

2. Tell students that a *character* is a person or animal that plays a role in a story and that characters in a story, like real people, have special qualities called *traits*. Point out that authors tell about characters' traits by describing what the characters look like, how they behave, and what the characters say or feel.

3. Retell the story of "The Three Little Pigs," or read aloud one of the standard versions listed under "Materials" above. Ask, "What words would you use to describe the wolf in this story?" As students make suggestions, write each word inside the outline of the wolf's head and ask, "What information or words in the story give you this impression of the wolf?"

4. Next, draw a second wolf outline next to the first. Read aloud *The True Story of the Three Little Pigs.* Ask, "What words would you use to describe the wolf in this story?" and list the words inside the outline. Again ask, "What information or words in the story gave you this impression?"

5. Point out that the words in the outlines tell about each wolf's character traits. Ask, "Are the character traits of the wolf in the first story the same as the character traits of the wolf in the second story? How are they different? Which wolf do you like better? Why?"

6. Ask students to look in their books for information or words that the author uses to reveal the traits of the main characters they are reading about.

As you take the Status of the Class, ask:
- Who is one of the main characters in your book?
- What are some of the character's traits? What does he look like? How is he behaving or feeling right now?
- What information or words does the author use to show you these character traits?

ADDED PRACTICE

- Suggest that students draw pictures of characters in their books. On lines or bubbles connected to the picture, students can write words or phrases the author uses to reveal the character's traits.

- Students can act out the part of the wolf in each version of "The Three Little Pigs." Discuss with students the words and actions they use to reveal each wolf's character traits.

MAIN IDEA

GRADE LEVEL : Intermediate (3-5)

OBJECTIVE : To help students identify the main idea in a piece of writing

MATERIALS : Any book you are currently reading to students, such as *Misty of Chincoteague* by Marguerite Henry (4.1); interesting action photo cut from a magazine

LESSON : **1.** Hold up an action photograph from a magazine. Ask students, "What is this photograph all about?" Discuss students' responses until you all agree on the main idea. Again, hold up the photo. This time ask students to give one or two details about the picture. Place the photo face down on a desk. After a few minutes, ask, "Who can tell me what that photo was about?" Point out that talking about what the photo was about (its *main idea),* along with some of the details, may have helped them understand and remember the photo.

2. Read aloud a paragraph or two from your current Read Aloud book, such as this selection from *Misty of Chincoteague.*

> "It's about Pony Penning Day," [Paul] blurted out.
> "How did it start?"
> "'Twas this-a-way," [Grandpa] said. "In the yesterdays, when their corn was laid by, folks on Chincoteague got to yearnin' fer a big hollerday. So they sails over to Assateague and rounds up all the wild ponies. 'Twas big sport."

Ask, "What is this part of the book about?" (Pony Penning Day) Write students' responses on the chalkboard. Explain that a *topic* is one or two words that explain what that part of the book is all about.

3. Next ask, "What is the most important idea about the topic?" (How Pony Penning Day started) Explain that the *main idea* is the most important idea about the topic.

4. Draw the pyramid shown below. In the top layer, write "Pony Penning Day." In the next layer, write "How Pony Penning Day Started." Then point to the layer on the bottom. Ask, "What are some details that tell more about the main idea?" Fill in the sections of that layer with details.

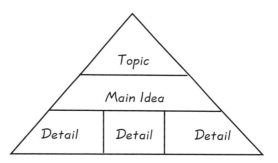

5. Ask students, "In the part of the book that I just read to you, where did you find the main idea?" (In the selection from *Misty*, the main idea is found in Paul's question at the beginning.) Tell students that the main idea also can be found in a sentence in the middle or end of a selection.

6. Review the following list of strategies for finding topics and main ideas. Then ask students to look for the topic and main ideas in their books.

◆ To find the topic, ask, "What is this book (or part of the book) all about?" If you can't find the topic immediately, look for an important word that is repeated often.

◆ To find the main idea, ask, "What is the most important idea about the topic?" Look for a sentence in the beginning, middle, or end of the book (or section of the book) that gives the most important idea.

◆ If you can't find a sentence that tells the main idea, make a list of important points and see what they all have in common. That idea will be the main idea.

◆ The main idea should cover all the important details in the book or section. Look for details that tell more about the main idea.

Continued on next page

STATUS OF THE CLASS FOLLOW-UP

As you take the Status of the Class, ask:

- Can you say in one or two words what the topic of this book (or this part of the book) is?
- What is the main idea?
- Where did you look to find the main idea?
- Can you name two important details from this book (or this part of the book)? Do the details support or tell more about the main idea?
- Give students short newspaper articles with the headlines cut off. Ask them to write a headline that clearly states the main idea of each article.

ADDED PRACTICE

- Suggest that students make parachutes for books they have read. First, have them use construction paper to make a small replica of the book cover. Then have them cut a parachute and thin strips from construction paper and connect the parachute to the book cover replica with the strips. Ask students to write their book's main idea on the parachute. On each of the connecting strips, they can write details that support the main idea. Hang the parachutes from the ceiling or post them on a bulletin board.

GENRE: FOLKTALES

GRADE LEVEL : Intermediate (3-5)

OBJECTIVE : To introduce folktales as a genre

MATERIALS : A traditional version of *Little Red Riding Hood,* such as that by Charles Perrault (4.7) or Trina Hyman (3.9); one or two alternative versions, such as *Lon Po Po: A Red Riding Hood Story from China* by Ed Young (3.9)

LESSON : **1.** Read or tell a traditional version of "Little Red Riding Hood." Ask, "Does anyone remember this story differently?" Discuss students' versions of the story.

2. Remind students that stories like "Little Red Riding Hood" are called *folktales.* Explain that a folktale is a story that is handed down from generation to generation by storytellers. At some point someone decides to write the story down and publish it. Tell students that although folktales are told in many different cultures, they tend to have common characteristics.

◆ The characters in the story are one-dimensional or "stock" characters—either all good (a fairy godmother, for example) or all bad (the wicked stepmother). Other stock characters are tricksters, such as Ananzi and Iktomi, and ne'er-do-wells, such as Jack in "Jack and the Beanstalk."

◆ Characters often have one goal, such as overcoming an evil force, marrying a prince or princess, or gaining fame or fortune. The plot consists of the character's attempts to reach that goal.

◆ Often there is an element of magic in the tale.

◆ Folktales often attempt to explain a natural occurrence or give a lesson. Good is almost always rewarded and evil is usually punished.

3. Read one of the alternative versions of "Little Red Riding Hood" and ask students to compare it to the first version. Review the list of common characteristics and ask which ones are found in the alternative version. Discuss why the tales may vary—

because of cultural differences, for example. Ask students which version they prefer and why.

4. Tell students that knowing the characteristics of folktales will help them enjoy and think critically about the tales they read on their own.

As you take the Status of the Class, ask:
- ◆ Have you read a folktale recently?
- ◆ Which characteristics of a folktale did you find in the story?
- ◆ Would you like to read other versions of the story or other stories from the same culture?

ADDED PRACTICE

- ◆ Encourage groups of students to perform a puppet play or skit based on a folktale they have read.

- ◆ Write the following chart on the chalkboard. With students, brainstorm a list of stock characters, plots, and settings based on folktales they know. Have students write an original folktale using at least one element from each column.

Characters:	_Plots:_	_Settings:_
Giant	Is kidnapped	Cave
Princess	Gets lost	Castle
Coyote	Finds magic object	Woods

DICTIONARY SKILLS

GRADE LEVEL   Intermediate (3-5)

OBJECTIVE   To help students learn to find the definitions and pronunciations of words in the dictionary

MATERIALS   Any book you are currently reading to students; student dictionaries

LESSON   You may wish to teach dictionary skills in three separate mini-lessons. If you have enough copies of the same dictionary, have students use the dictionaries during the lessons. If you have limited copies or many different editions, give students ample time after each lesson to look through dictionaries and practice the skills they have learned.

Day One   **1.** On the chalkboard, write a sentence that contains an unfamiliar word and few context clues, for example, "It was a good idea, but where would we find the *capital?*"

2. Ask, "What do you do if you run into a word you don't know while you are reading?" Discuss students' suggestions. Conclude the discussion by saying, "Today we're going to begin talking about how to figure out the meaning and pronunciation of a word by looking it up in a dictionary."

3. Write the alphabet horizontally across the chalkboard and roughly divide it into three parts:

a b c d e f g   h i j k l m n o p   q r s t u v w x y z

Hold up a dictionary, open it to a page in the last third of the book, and say, "Let's say I want to use a dictionary to figure out what the word *capital* means. Would this be a good place to start looking?" Point out that since the first letter in *capital* appears in the first part of the alphabet, and the dictionary is arranged in alphabetical order, it makes sense to start searching in the first part of the dictionary.

4. Open the dictionary to the c section and ask, "Now what?" Point out that because there are many words in the dictionary that begin with the letter *c,* you have to look at the letters that come afterwards in order to narrow your search. If necessary, review alphabetizing rules.

5. Turn to the page where the word *capital* is found. Point to the guide words at the top of the page and say, "Here is another way the dictionary helps you find words quickly." Explain that guide words show the first and last words listed on the page. On the board, write the guide words for the page on which *capital* is found, for example, *canvas* and *capsule.* Between the two words, write *capital.* Ask, "Does *capital* come after *canvas?* Does *capital* come before *capsule?*"

6. Remind students that the words in dark type on a dictionary page are called entry words. Run your finger down the list of entry words on the page until you come to *capital,* and then shout, "Eureka! We found it!"

7. Tell students that in the next mini-lesson they will learn how to use the dictionary to help them figure out the meaning of a word.

Day Two

1. Write a dictionary entry, such as the following, on the chalk-board or a reproducible sheet. Be sure to use a word that has at least two meanings.

capital \kăp′ ĭ tl\ —noun, capitals 1. A city where the govern-ment is located: We will visit the capital on our trip. 2. Money or property: She finally has enough capital to start her own business. 3. A capital letter: Did you start each sentence with a capital?
—adjective 1. Most important: a capital city. 2. Calling for punishment by death: Murder is a capital offense.

2. Point to each part of the dictionary entry as you describe it and explain its purpose:
   ◆ *Entry words* are usually listed without endings such as *s, ed,* and *ing.*

- The *pronunciation respelling* uses symbols to show how the entry word is pronounced.
- The *part of speech* tells how the word is used in a sentence.
- The *definition* gives the meaning of the entry word. If the word has more than one definition, the definitions are numbered.
- A *sample sentence* gives an example of how the word may be used in a sentence.

3. Rewrite or point to the sentence used in the previous lesson. Point to each definition in the entry and ask, "Does this definition make sense in this sentence? Why or why not?"

4. Tell students that in the next mini-lesson they will learn how to use a dictionary to help them figure out how to pronounce a word.

Day Three

1. Give students dictionaries to share, or copy the pronunciation key from a dictionary onto the chalkboard or a reproducible sheet.

2. Write the pronunciation respelling from the previous lesson on the chalkboard, for example, \ kăp′ ĭ tl \. Ask, "Have any of you ever written a message in code?" Explain that dictionaries use a kind of code to help readers pronounce words. Ask a volunteer to read the word written in "dictionary code" on the board.

3. Tell students that every entry in a dictionary includes a special spelling given in parentheses. This spelling shows how the word is broken into syllables and uses special letters and symbols to show sounds. It also includes accent marks, which tell you which syllable get the most stress or force when you say the word.

4. Tell students that dictionaries have a key to the special spelling code on every page. Point to the pronunciation key on the board or in students' dictionaries. Explain that the pronunciation key tells how to pronounce the letters and symbols given in the special spelling.

5. Onto the board, copy a pronunciation respelling for a second word and ask students to use the pronunciation key and the following steps to figure out how to pronounce the word.

- For most *consonants,* use the sound that you usually use for the letter. Letters that have more than one sound may be represented by a different letter (such as *k* for the hard *c* sound) or a combination of letters (*zh* for the *s* in *vision).*
- *Vowels* usually have special symbols. Look in the pronunciation key to see how to pronounce each symbol.
- If a word has two or more *accent marks,* place the most stress on the syllable with the darker mark and a lighter stress on the syllable with the lighter mark.

6. Tell students that knowing how to use a dictionary will help them figure out new words they come across in their books.

STATUS OF THE CLASS FOLLOW-UP

As you take the Status of the Class, ask:

- Have you come across any words that you don't know the meaning of or that you're not sure how to pronounce?
- Can you show me how you would look up this word in the dictionary?
- Which meaning of this word makes sense in this sentence?
- How do you pronounce this word?

ADDED PRACTICE

- Suggest that small groups of students play the game Fictionary. In this game, one player chooses an unknown word from the dictionary and writes the real definition (just one meaning) on a slip of paper. The other players write mock definitions in "dictionary-ese" on slips of paper. The player who chose the word reads aloud all of the responses. Players who identify the correct definition get a point. Whenever someone chooses an incorrect definition, the player who selected the word gets a point.

  You can vary the difficulty of this game by requiring players to give the word's pronunciation or part of speech, as well as its definition.

- Give students copies of a pronunciation key and have them write messages to each other in "pronunciation code."

- Give students a list of spelling or vocabulary words, and have them time how long it takes to look up each word in the dictionary.

- Compile a list of related words, such as *persimmon* and *soursop.* Have students use a dictionary to find how the two words are alike. (For example, a persimmon and a soursop are both fruits.) Encourage students to create lists of their own.

USING CONTEXT CLUES

GRADE LEVEL : Middle School (6-8)

OBJECTIVE : To help students use context clues to figure out unfamiliar words

MATERIALS : Any book you are currently reading to students, such as *Redwall* by Brian Jacques (6.8)

LESSON : **1.** Read aloud a sentence, preferably from your current Read To book, that contains an unfamiliar word, for example, "Now let's see, a good *haversack* to carry it all, enough food and drink, ah, and some candied chestnuts for you, my friend," from *Redwall*. Ask, "If you see an unfamiliar word like *haversack* when you're reading, what are some ways you can figure out the word?"

2. As you discuss students' suggestions, focus on the use of context clues. Reread the sentence and ask, "What other words in that sentence can help you figure out the word *haversack*?"

3. Tell students that context clues can help readers figure out meanings of words in the following situations:

◆ When a familiar word has two or more possible meanings:

I have to <u>wind</u> this old watch.

The <u>wind</u> blew the roof off the house.

◆ When a word is completely unfamiliar:

The magician didn't really make the boy disappear—it was just a <u>hoax</u>.

4. Explain to students that good readers have strategies for using context clues to figure out unfamiliar words. List the strategies on the chalkboard as you discuss each one.

◆ Look for *clues,* such as synonyms, antonyms, and examples:

She was more than <u>angry</u>, she was <u>exasperated</u>. (synonym)

We needed a <u>large</u> hall. We would never fit in that <u>minuscule</u> room. (antonym)

<u>Charlatans</u> like that <u>fake doctor</u> should be run out of town. (example)

♦ Use *common sense*. What else is happening in the story? Who says the word, to whom, and why?

The team <u>lost last week's game</u> by a score of 42 to 0. I hope they can put that <u>debacle</u> behind them.

The wounded general was <u>borne</u> on a plank <u>by his loyal men</u>.

♦ Look up the word in the *dictionary* and think about how the definition fits into the sentence.

5. Ask students to look in their books for two unfamiliar words and to be prepared to tell how they used the context to figure out each word's meaning.

STATUS OF THE CLASS FOLLOW-UP

As you take the Status of the Class, ask:
- ♦ Have you run into any unfamiliar words in your book?
- ♦ Did you use the context to help you figure out the meaning of the word? What strategies did you use?
- ♦ What could you do if there were no clues in the sentence to help you figure out the meaning of the word? (Look in the dictionary. Rely on common sense.)

ADDED PRACTICE

- ♦ Have students form small groups, each with a dictionary. Each student reads a paragraph from his book that contains unfamiliar words. Members of the group predict the meaning of the words and check their answers in the dictionary.

- ♦ Have students choose an unfamiliar word from the dictionary and write a sentence, giving the word the strongest context possible. If necessary, review the strategies discussed in this lesson so that students can use them as they write. Have students read their sentences aloud and ask others to predict the meaning of the unfamiliar word.

DRAWING CONCLUSIONS

GRADE LEVEL Middle School (6-8)

OBJECTIVE To help students use the skill of drawing conclusions to improve comprehension

MATERIALS An empty box; a "fractured fairy tale," such as *The Frog Prince Continued* by Jon Scieszka (3.6)

LESSON **1.** Present this scenario: "Every morning, you ride your bike to deliver papers along your paper route. This morning you looked out the window and saw that it was pouring down rain. What was your conclusion?"
- You would skip delivering papers this morning.
- You would put on rain gear and ride the route as usual.
- You would ask your mom or dad to drive you in the car.

2. Tell students that they draw conclusions every day. Add that they also draw conclusions every time they read a book or hear a story. Ask a volunteer to give a brief synopsis of the fairy tale about the Frog Prince. (A princess kisses a frog, and he turns into a handsome prince.) Ask, "What's the conclusion that people draw from this story?" (that the prince and princess will live happily ever after)

3. Ask, "Why do you think people draw that conclusion?" Students' answers might include:
- Princes and princesses usually fall in love with each other.
- The prince hated being a frog.
- Princes and princesses are meant to get married and live happily ever after.

4. Introduce the book *The Frog Prince Continued* and ask two students to act out the roles of the princess and the prince, using the dialogue from the first page:
> PRINCESS: Stop sticking your tongue out like that! And I would prefer that you not hop around on the furniture.
> PRINCE: How come you never want to go down to the pond anymore?

5. Ask, "What conclusions can you draw from this conversation?" (That the prince and princess are not happy; that they are fed up with each other.)

6. Discuss the different conclusions that were drawn from the same story. Point out that drawing sound conclusions involves the following:

- Paying attention to a character's appearance, conversation, and tone of voice.
- Noting important facts and actions.
- Thinking not just about one detail but many details.
- "Reading between the lines," or applying your own experience and judgment to the facts given.

7. Remind students that taking time to draw conclusions about what they read will make their reading more fun and interesting.

STATUS OF THE CLASS FOLLOW-UP

As you take the Status of the Class, ask:

- What conclusions can you draw about this character or event?
- What facts or reasons support your conclusion? Do you know that all those facts are true, or are you making some assumptions?
- Do you think the author (or another character) has come to the same conclusion? Why or why not?
- Is your conclusion the only reasonable one? What is another reasonable conclusion someone might draw?

ADDED PRACTICE

- Cut off the last frame of a comic strip, and post the rest of the strip on a bulletin board. Have students write what happens in the last frame and give their reasons for drawing that conclusion.

- Encourage students who have read the same book to make a list of items that one of the characters might carry in his or her backpack or suitcase. Have students exchange lists and guess the identity of the character by drawing conclusions based on the contents of the backpack and their knowledge of the character.

FACT AND OPINION

GRADE LEVEL   Middle School (6-8)

OBJECTIVE   To help students distinguish between fact and opinion

MATERIALS   Any nonfiction book you are currently reading to students, such as *Volcano: The Eruption and Healing of Mount St. Helens* (7.0) by Patricia Lauber.

LESSON

1. On the board, write two statements that are related to a current event or nonfiction book that you are reading to the class. One sentence should be a statement of fact; the other should be a statement of opinion, for example:

> *I don't think the eruption of Mount St. Helens was terribly devastating.*

> *The eruption of Mount St. Helens did not cause as many deaths as the eruption of Mt. Pele.*

2. Point to each statement, and ask, "Is this a statement of fact or opinion?" Remind students that statements of fact can be proven true or false, whereas statements of opinion cannot be proven true or false. When students identify a statement as *fact,* ask, "How could you check this fact?" When they identify a statement as *opinion,* ask, "If you agreed with this statement, would that make it a fact?"

3. With students, create a list of clue words that can help them identify statements of opinion, for example:

> *think, believe   good, better, best*
> *suppose, wonder   bad, worse, worst*
> *should, ought   right, wrong*

4. Write a sentence that combines both fact and opinion, such as:

> *Mount St. Helens, which erupted in 1980, was the worst disaster ever.*

Ask, "Which part of this sentence is fact? Which part is opinion?"

5. Now write on the board two additional statements. One should be an incorrect fact. The other should be a strongly supported opinion.

> *The eruption of Mount St. Helens caused more deaths than the eruption of Mt. Vesuvius.*

> *I don't think the eruption of Mount St. Helens was terribly devastating because nature regenerated itself so quickly.*

6. Ask whether the sentences are statements of fact or opinion. If necessary, point out the following:
- Statements of fact can be correct or incorrect.
- Statements of opinion can be well supported or not well supported. You may agree with them or disagree with them.

7. Tell students that they should look for statements of fact and opinion as they read their books. They should be prepared to tell you why the statement is a fact or an opinion.

STATUS OF THE CLASS FOLLOW-UP

As you take the Status of the Class, ask:
- Can you find a statement of fact or opinion in your book? Read it aloud to me. Is this a statement of fact or opinion?
- What is it about this sentence that makes you think it is a statement of fact (or opinion)?
- How might you prove this statement true or false?

ADDED PRACTICE

- Have students cut out advertisements from magazines and newspapers. Have them mount the ads on construction paper and label each statement *fact* or *opinion*.

- Each day, write one statement on the chalkboard, such as "Hamburgers are better for you than hotdogs." Discuss with students whether they think the statement is one of fact or opinion and why.

FIGURES OF SPEECH

GRADE LEVEL : Middle School (6-8)

OBJECTIVE : To help students recognize figures of speech

MATERIALS : Any book you are currently reading to students, such as *Hatchet* by Gary Paulsen (6.1)

LESSON : You may wish to teach figures of speech in four separate mini-lessons.

Day One : **1.** On the chalkboard, write a sentence that contains a simile. If possible, choose a sentence from your current Read To book, for example, "The sparks poured like a golden waterfall" from *Hatchet.*

2. Tell students that one way authors create pictures in readers' minds is by using figurative language, or figures of speech. Explain that figures of speech convey meanings that may be different from the definitions of the words they use, and they often make ideas vivid for readers.

3. Read aloud the sentence on the board. Underline the word *like* and say, "Some figures of speech create images by comparing two unlike things. A *simile* uses the words *like* or *as* to make a comparison." Ask students what two things are being compared in the sentence on the board. (sparks and a waterfall)

4. Ask students to help you brainstorm a list of similes, such as *busy as a bee, works like a horse,* and *cheeks like roses.*

5. Point out that some similes, like many of those on the list, are so overused that the images have lost their impact. Ask students to suggest less commonly used alternatives for some of the similes on the list.

6. Have students look through their books to find one or two examples of similes to read aloud and discuss.

Day Two

1. Briefly review how figures of speech are used to create images. Remind students that a simile is a figure of speech that makes a comparison using the words *like* and *as.*

2. On the chalkboard, write a sentence containing a metaphor, such as "His legs were liquid springs" from *Hatchet.* Tell students that *metaphors* also compare two unlike things, but they do not use *like* or *as.* Ask, "What two things are compared in this metaphor?" (legs and springs)

3. Write a simple sentence, such as "Her voice was <u>nice</u>" on the chalkboard. Ask students to suggest ways to rewrite the sentence using a metaphor. List students' suggestions on the board and discuss the comparison made in each metaphor.

4. Have students look through their books to find one or two examples of metaphors to read aloud and discuss.

Day Three

1. Briefly review the definitions for simile and metaphor. On the chalkboard, write a sentence containing an example of personification, such as "He fed the hungry fire" from *Hatchet.*

2. Tell students that a figure of speech in which an author gives human qualities to something that is not human is called *personification.* Read aloud the sentence on the board and ask, "What human quality has the author given fire in this sentence?" (hunger)

3. Remind students that many of the stories they read when they were younger contained personified objects or animals. Briefly brainstorm a list of examples such as Peter Rabbit, The Little Engine That Could, and Winnie the Pooh.

4. Ask volunteers to choose an object in the room and make up a sentence about the object that uses personification. Discuss the human qualities given to the objects.

Continued on next page

Day Four

1. Write the following list on the chalkboard.

> _Tell me what happened._
> _Spill the beans._
> _Let the cat out of the bag._
> _Shed some light on the subject._

2. Tell students that each of the expressions listed under _Tell me what happened_ is an _idiom_—an expression whose meaning can't be understood from the ordinary meanings of the words. Ask, "Do you know any other idioms that mean 'Tell me what happened'?" Add students' suggestions to the list.

3. Next, ask, "How many idioms can you think of that use the word _throw_? (throw in the towel, throw a party, throw a fit) List the idioms on the board and ask volunteers to use each one in a sentence.

4. Have students look through their books to find one or two examples of an idiom. Have students read aloud the sentence containing the idiom and then reread the sentence replacing the idiom with another word or phrase that has the same meaning.

STATUS OF THE CLASS FOLLOW-UP

As you take the Status of the Class, ask:
- Have you come across any figures of speech while reading? Can you read an example to me?
- What kind of figure of speech is your example?
- What is the comparison that this figure of speech makes? (Or, what does this idiom mean?)

ADDED PRACTICE

- Divide a bulletin board into four sections and label the sections _Similes, Metaphors, Personification, Idioms._ Have students look through newspapers and magazines for examples of each figure of speech, cut out the examples, and post them under the labels on the bulletin board.

◆ Pair up students and challenge each pair to create a dialogue using only idioms. Have students act out their dialogues and then "translate" them by giving the meanings of the idioms.

◆ Sports writing often contains a great deal of figurative language. Copy a particularly florid passage onto the chalkboard or a reproducible sheet. Have students rewrite the passage replacing the figures of speech with literal language. Discuss what happens to the writing when the figurative language is taken out.

GENRE: MYSTERY

GRADE LEVEL Middle School (6-8)

OBJECTIVE To introduce mystery as a genre

MATERIALS Any mystery you are currently reading to students, such as *The Westing Game* by Ellen Raskin (6.3)

LESSON **1.** Ask students, "What is a mystery?" On the chalkboard, record key words or bits of information from the discussion, such as "something we don't understand," "a puzzle," "a crime that has to be solved."

2. Ask, "What makes for a good mystery story?" During the discussion, emphasize the following points:
- A mystery may be realistic, involving ordinary circumstances and settings, or it may be a fantasy, in which the author creates strange worlds and exaggerated characters.
- The author carefully constructs a mystery's *plot* to emphasize a problem that needs to be solved. Often the plot involves a sequence of unexplained events.
- Most mysteries maintain a suspenseful *mood*. A scary *setting*, such as a deep woods on a moonless night, contributes to this mood.
- Mysteries usually have memorable *characters*. The reader must scrutinize each of these to figure out who is responsible for the crime or mysterious behavior.

3. Tell students that good mystery writers usually plant clues in their stories to help readers predict the outcome of the mystery. Keeping track of these clues can make the story easier to follow and the mystery itself easier to solve. On the chalkboard, draw a large chart like the one on the opposite page for the mystery you are currently reading to students. Encourage volunteers to add information to the chart day by day as you continue to read the mystery aloud.

THE WESTING GAME		
SUSPECT	CLUES	DID SHE/HE DO IT?
Otis Amber	Carries a revolver. Needs money.	Possible murderer
Grace Windsor Wexler	Had to abandon family when married. Sam Westing's niece. Would inherit money.	Top suspect
Bertha Crow	Odd secretive habits. Has bad feelings about Westinghouse. Thinks Sam Westing is evil.	Probably not
Turtle	Was in Westing House the night Sam Westing was murdered. Likes money. Plays the stock market. Young.	Probably not

4. Tell the class that being aware of how the plot, characterization, and setting of a mystery all add to its suspenseful mood will help them enjoy and think critically about the mysteries they read on their own.

STATUS OF THE CLASS FOLLOW-UP

As you take the Status of the Class, ask:
- Have you read a mystery recently? What was the problem that needed to be solved?
- How did the author create suspense?
- Were you pleased with the way the mystery was solved? Why or why not?
- Would you like to read another mystery by this author?

If the student is currently reading a mystery, ask:
- What is the mystery that needs to be solved in this book?
- What is the setting of the story? How does the setting affect what's going on in the mystery?
- Which character do you find the most interesting? Why?
- How do you think the mystery will be solved? What are the clues that make you think that?

Continued on next page

ADDED PRACTICE

♦ Encourage students to make a chart for the mystery they are currently reading and use it to list clues and predictions.

♦ After students have finished reading their books, suggest that they imagine they are lawyers. Have them write a defense for the most suspicious or villainous character in the book. Groups of students who have read the same book also can set up mock courtroom trials based on evidence from the book.

GENRE: HISTORICAL FICTION

GRADE LEVEL : Middle School (6-8)

OBJECTIVE : To help students identify the elements of historical fiction

MATERIALS : Any historical fiction you are currently reading to students, such as *I, Juan de Pareja* by Elizabeth Borton de Trevino (7.9), and a contemporary novel such as *Maniac Magee* by Jerry Spinelli (5.0)

LESSON : **1.** Hold up an example of historical fiction that you have read to the class, such as *I, Juan de Pareja*. Ask students if the novel was set in the past or in the present. Then ask if the events and/or characters in the story are real or fictional. As you discuss the novel, you may wish to include the following points:

◆ In historical fiction, some characters may be real and some may be fictional.
◆ The story is set in a specific time and place in the past.
◆ Real events may be mixed with fictional events.
◆ Descriptions of events, places, and characters are in keeping with the historical setting of the novel.

2. Remind students that novels like *I, Juan de Pareja* are referred to as "historical fiction." Establish when and where the novel is set and ask, "What do you learn about seventeenth-century Spain by reading this book? List students' observations on the chalkboard.

3. Ask students to recall a work of contemporary fiction they recently have read, such as *Maniac Magee*. On the chalkboard, draw a chart like the one on the next page and ask students to help you fill in the blanks.

	I, Juan de Pareja	Maniac Magee
Time		
Place		
Main Character		
Problem		

4. Ask, "How does a historical novel like *I, Juan de Pareja* differ from a contemporary novel like *Maniac Magee*?" To guide students' thinking, you might ask such questions as:
- What makes each story realistic?
- Why is one historical and the other not?
- Which parts of each story are true? Which parts were made up by the author?

5. Tell students that understanding the historical context of books will help them better understand and appreciate what they read.

STATUS OF THE CLASS FOLLOW-UP

As you take the Status of the Class, ask:
- Does the story you are reading have a historical or contemporary setting?
- If the story is historical, when and where is it set?
- Does the character in the novel remind you of a contemporary character? How?
- Has this novel taught you anything interesting about a different period in history?

ADDED PRACTICE

◆ Have students write a diary entry for a character in a historical novel they have read. The entry should include a date and references to historical events happening at the time.

◆ Suggest that students create a "Wanted" poster for a character in a historical novel. Remind them to include a physical description of the character, when and where the character was last seen, and information about the character's misdeed or what might have been viewed in that time period as a crime.

GENRE: BIOGRAPHY

GRADE LEVEL   Middle School (6-8)

OBJECTIVE   To introduce biography as a genre

MATERIALS   Any biography, such as *Lincoln, A Photobiography* by Russell Freedman (6.3)

LESSON   **1.** Remind students that nonfiction books tell about real people, places, things, or events. Discuss what students know about the nonfiction genre called *biography.* As you discuss biographies, emphasize the following points:

- A biography is the story of a person's life told by someone else.
- The subjects of biographies usually have done something significant or their lives offer lessons we can learn from.
- Facts in a biography must be accurate; authors get the facts from various sources, including historical records and letters. If a subject is still living, the author may interview him or her.
- A biography consists of more than just facts. An author has to interpret facts and make judgments, too. This is why two authors writing about the same subject might offer very different interpretations of the same person.
- Details about everyday life make the subject of a biography come alive for the reader.

2. Tell students the title of your chosen book and, if necessary, the name of the person about whom the biography is written. Ask students what they already know about the person. Briefly record this information as well as any questions they have about the subject in a large K-W-L chart as shown.

ABRAHAM LINCOLN

What We Know   *What We Want to Know*   *What We Learned*

---

3. If the book contains an author's biography, read it aloud. Ask:
- What do you think the author's purpose was for writing about this person?
- Is the author especially qualified to write about this person?

4. Read a brief passage from the book. After you read the passage, ask students if they have learned anything new about the subject. Record their responses in the chart.

5. Choose a fact from the "What We Learned" column on the chart and ask, "Where do you think the author got this information?" Note any source given in the book. Then ask students to speculate about the author's purpose for including the information. Did the author want to liven up the story? Did he want to underscore a particular character trait? Tell students that asking questions like these will help them think critically about biographies they read on their own.

STATUS OF THE CLASS FOLLOW-UP

As you take the Status of the Class, ask:
- Have you read a biography recently? Who was it about?
- What do you think the author's purpose was for writing the biography? What about the story made you think that?
- What was one thing you learned from the biography?

If the student is currently reading a biography, ask:
- What kind of person is the subject? How do you know?
- Why do you think the author wrote about the subject?
- Do you think the author is giving a fair and accurate portrait of the subject? Why or why not?

ADDED PRACTICE

- Have students create a time line for their biographical subject's life. If the subject is a historical figure, suggest that they include major historical events that took place during the subject's lifetime as well.

- Have students divide a sheet of paper into two columns. In one column, have them list their biographical subject's character traits. On the other side, have them record sentences or facts from the biography that illustrate each trait.

Note Taking

GRADE LEVEL Middle School (6-8)

OBJECTIVE To help students use the skill of note taking to understand and remember text

MATERIALS A nonfiction book related to a current theme of study, such as *Sharks and Other Monsters of the Deep* by Phillip Steele (7.0)

LESSON **1.** Ask students, "Do you ever make a list or jot down notes outside of school? When and why do you do it?" Discuss students' responses and point out that many of their reasons for taking notes outside of school also are good reasons for taking notes as they read, for example:

- ◆ To keep track of or organize information
- ◆ To remember what they've read

Explain that there also are two specific purposes for taking notes in school:

- ◆ To prepare for a test
- ◆ To gather information for a report

2. Hold up the nonfiction book and say, "Suppose I am reading this book for a report that I'm writing on _____ [whatever the subject is, sharks in our example]. Here are the steps I would follow to take notes on this book." Draw a large image of a note-card on the chalkboard. As you describe the following steps, record examples on the card.

Step 1. Think: Before I begin reading, I mentally review what I already know about the subject and what I want to learn.

Step 2. Survey: I look through the book, noticing headings and subheadings. These tell me what ideas are being explained.

Step 3. Read: I read entire paragraphs or complete sections, making sure I understand them, before I begin taking notes.

Step 4. Write: I pick out only the most important ideas or the information for which I specifically am looking. Instead of copying exactly what's in the book, I write the ideas in my own words.

Step 5. Review: I read over my notes to see if they are clear. If they are not, I add more information. If I am writing a report, I also make sure I have jotted down the title of the book, its author, and the page on which I found the information.

3. Tell students that they can pause and take notes any time they want to keep track of information or to help themselves remember what they have read. Ask, "What kind of information might you take notes about if you were reading fiction?" (names of characters, setting, main ideas and supporting details) Tell students that they can add to or change their notes as they read.

STATUS OF THE CLASS FOLLOW-UP

As you take the Status of the Class, ask:
- ◆ What reason could you have for taking notes on this book?
- ◆ If you were taking notes on this book, what information would you include?

ADDED PRACTICE

- ◆ Ask students to take notes on a book they are currently reading. After students have taken notes, suggest that they use colored markers to organize the notes. For instance, if they have taken notes about polar bears, they might use a green marker to underline notes about polar bear habitat, a red marker to underline notes about diet, and a yellow marker to underline notes about behavior.

- ◆ Students can use a graphic like the one shown to record their notes.

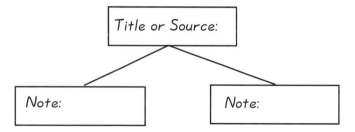

ANALOGIES

GRADE LEVEL Middle School (6-8)

OBJECTIVE To introduce students to the analogy format used on standardized tests

MATERIALS Any book you are currently reading to students, such as *Belle Prater's Boy* by Ruth White (5.7)

LESSON

1. Tell students that you have a word puzzle to show them. On the chalkboard, write an analogy based on your current Read To book, such as, "Gypsy is to her father as Woodrow is to ____," from *Belle Prater's Boy*. Ask students how they would complete the sentence and list their responses on the board. Do not give the correct answer at this time.

2. Remind students that good readers constantly make connections and analyze how things are related. Tell them that one way this type of thinking is strengthened and tested is through the use of *analogies.* On the chalkboard, underneath the sentence you have just written, write "*Up* is to *down* as *over* is to ____." Tell students that both sentences on the chalkboard are analogies. Point out that these analogies consist of two pairs of words and that the words in both pairs are related in the same way. Ask, "How is *up* related to *down*?" (It's the opposite.) Then ask, "What word has the same relationship to *over* as *up* has to *down*?" (under)

3. Write a series of analogies on the chalkboard, using as many different relationships as possible. Ask volunteers to describe the relationship between the first pair of words and then complete the sentence.
- *Ear* is to *hear* as *nose* is to _____. (object and action; smell)
- *Penny* is to *dollar* as *centimeter* is to ____. (part and whole; meter)
- *Paintbrush* is to *painter* as *camera* is to ___. (object and user; photographer)
- *Ice* is to *cold* as *fire* is to ___. (object and characteristic; hot)

4. Rewrite one or two of these analogies in standard test notation (ear: hear :: nose: smell). Tell students that this is another way of writing an analogy. (If your students have studied ratios and proportions in mathematics, this format may already be familiar to them.) Ask volunteers to rewrite the rest of the analogies on the board in standard notation.

5. Go back to the analogy you first wrote on the board. (*Gypsy* is to her *father* as *Woodrow* is to ____.) Ask students which of the recorded answers makes sense and why. Tell students that being aware of relationships will help them better understand what they read.

STATUS OF THE CLASS FOLLOW-UP

As you take the Status of the Class, ask:
◆ What is the relationship between these two characters? Can you think of another set of characters that have the same relationship?
◆ Can you create an analogy that relates this book to another book you've read?

ADDED PRACTICE

◆ Have students create analogies, leaving the last word blank and writing an answer key on a separate piece of paper. Students can exchange papers, complete the analogies, and then check one anothers' work.

◆ Suggest that students cut pictures out of old magazines to create pictorial analogies. The analogies may be simple (girl : woman :: boy : man) or complex (extensive : restricted :: enlarge : diminish).

WORDS FROM GREEK AND LATIN

GRADE LEVEL : High School (9-12)

OBJECTIVE : To help students decode words and figure out their meaning by recognizing Greek and Latin word parts

MATERIALS : List of words from Greek and Latin (page 70)

LESSON : **1.** Remind students that the English language contains many words and word parts borrowed from other languages, and ask volunteers to give examples.

2. If one of the examples given contains a Greek or Latin word part, write that word on the chalkboard. Also write the words *philanthropist* and *translucent.* Tell students that many English words have word parts borrowed from Greek and Latin. Explain that knowing the meaning of these common word parts can help them figure out unfamiliar words.

3. Ask volunteers to give their definitions of the word *philanthropist.* To confirm the definition, point out that *philanthropist* contains two Greek word parts, *philo-,* meaning "loving," and *anthr,* meaning "human."

4. Follow the same procedure for the word *translucent.* Confirm students' definitions by pointing out the Latin word parts, *trans,* meaning "across," and *luc,* meaning "light."

5. Write *philo, anthr, trans,* and *luc* across the top of the chalkboard. Help students brainstorm other words that have the same Greek and Latin word parts.

philo	*anthr*	*trans*	*luc*
philosopher	anthropology	transportation	lucid
philharmonic	misanthrope	transcend	elucidate

6. Hand out the list of words from Greek and Latin. Ask students to look over the lists and then look in their books to find two words that contain Greek or Latin word parts.

STATUS OF THE CLASS FOLLOW-UP

As you take the Status of the Class, ask:

◆ Have you found any words that contain Greek or Latin word parts?

◆ What is the meaning of the word part?

◆ Do you know the meaning of the word as a whole? If not, can you use what you know about the meaning of the word part to predict the meaning of the word itself?

ADDED PRACTICE

◆ Pairs of students can use the dictionary and the list of words from Greek and Latin to create riddles for one another to solve, such as:

What word contains the word part *ridi* and means "to make fun of"?

Satisfy, *saturate*, and *satiate* all have the word part *sat*. What does *sat* mean?

◆ Have students use word parts found in words from their books to create word webs. Suggest that they write the word part and its meaning in a circle in the center of the web. In the outer circles, have them write words containing that word part.

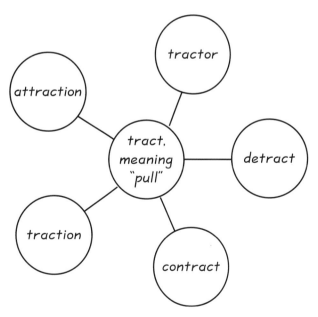

WORDS FROM GREEK AND LATIN

Word Part	Meaning	Examples
act	do	action, activist, react
anni, annu, enni	year	anniversary, annual, centennial
ast	star	asterisk, astronaut, astronomy
aud	hear	audience, audition, auditorium
cred	believe	credit, credulous, incredible
cycl	circle, wheel	bicycle, cycle, cyclone, cyclops
dent, dont	tooth	dentist, denture, orthodontist
duc, duct	lead	conduct, induct, produce
fac	make, do	facsimile, factory, manufacture
fed, fid	faith	confidence, federal, fidelity
graph	write	autograph, photograph, telegraph
ject	throw	objection, projection, reject
jud	judge	judicial, judicious, prejudice
lib	free	liberty, liberal, library
lit	letter	alliteration, literal, literary
man	hand	maneuver, manipulate, manual
mis, mit	send	missile, submit, transmit
meter	measure	metric, perimeter, thermometer
mob, mot	move	automobile, motor, promote
ped	foot	pedal, pedestrian, pedestal
phon	sound	phonograph, symphony, telephone
photo	light	photography, photosynthesis, telephoto
poly	many	polygamy, polyarchy, polygon
pop	people	populace, population, popular
port	carry	import, portable, transport
pos	place	deposit, position, repose
put	think	computer, deputy, reputation
rupt	break	abrupt, interrupt, rupture
sat	enough	insatiable, satisfy, saturate
scop	see	microscope, periscope, telescope
scrib, scrip	write	scribble, script, transcript
sim	like	similar, simile, simulate
soph	wise	philosopher, sophisticated, sophomore
spec	see	inspect, spectacle, spectator
therm	heat	thermal, thermometer, thermos
tract	pull	attraction, detract, tractor
uni	one	unique, unity, universe
vers, vert	turn	convert, reverse, versatile
vis, vid	see	evidence, video, vision

POINT OF VIEW

GRADE LEVEL : High School (9-12)

OBJECTIVE : To help students identify an author's point of view

MATERIALS : Any book written in the first-person point of view, such as *Catherine, Called Birdie* by Karen Cushman (7.4), and any book written in the third-person point of view, such as *The Trumpeter of Krakow* by Eric Kelly (8.1)

LESSON : **1.** Ask a student to briefly describe a recent school or sporting event. Then have a second student give her version of the same event. Ask, "How were these two descriptions alike? How were they different?"

2. Point out that all stories are written from a certain perspective or point of view. Explain that the point of view greatly affects the way the story is told and influences the reader's understanding of the characters and events.

3. Tell students that there are two main points of view, first person and third person, named after the personal pronouns used to tell the story. Read aloud a short selection written in the first-person point of view, such as this one from *Catherine, Called Birdie:*

> I am in disgrace today. Grown quite weary with my embroidery, with my pricked fingers and tired eyes and sore back, I kicked it down the stairs to the hall, where the dogs fought and slobbered over it, so I took the soggy mess and threw it to the pigs.

4. Ask, "What point of view is this written in? (the first person) How do you know?" (the use of *I*) Discuss the advantages and disadvantages of hearing a story from the first person point of view, and include the following points:
   ◆ The first-person point of view is intimate and emotionally powerful. The reader experiences events along with the narrator.

◆ The first-person point of view is "limited" by the fact that the reader observes events and characters through the eyes of only one character, who may or may not be accurate in her perceptions.

5. Next, read a selection from a story written in the third-person point of view, such as this one from *The Trumpeter of Krakow:*

> Joseph, however, was at that age when no sky remains long clouded. His heart had been beating fast with excitement ever since the sight of the city's towers had loomed before them in the early morning, and his legs had been itching to get out of the wagon and explore the place.

6. Ask, "What point of view is this written in? (the third person) How do you know?" (the use of *Joseph* and *his*) Tell students that third-person point of view can be one of two types:
◆ Omniscient third-person point of view: The narrator describes the thoughts and feelings of all characters.
◆ Limited third-person point of view: Even though the work is written in the third person, the narrator tells the story mainly through the eyes of one character.

7. Remind students that the narrator is *not* the same as the author and that there is no "best" point of view for all stories. Explain that an author chooses a point of view to serve a particular purpose.

8. Have students look through their books for examples of each point of view, and ask volunteers to read their examples aloud.

STATUS OF THE CLASS FOLLOW-UP

As you take the Status of the Class, ask:
◆ In which point of view is your book written?
◆ What tells you that it is written in that point of view?
◆ Why do you think the author chose to write in this point of view?

ADDED PRACTICE

◆ Have students choose a brief selection from their books and rewrite it in a different point of view. Discuss the advantages and disadvantages of each point of view.

◆ Post a magazine picture or a print of a painting that shows a number of different people engaged in an activity. Have students write a few paragraphs about the picture in either the first-person or limited third-person point of view. Compare the information each point of view gives the reader about the picture.

SUMMARIZING

GRADE LEVEL : High School (9-12)

OBJECTIVE : To help students use the skill of summarizing to improve comprehension

MATERIALS : Any fiction and nonfiction books you are currently reading to the class; television listings or bestseller lists with plot synopses

LESSON : **1.** Read aloud several examples from the TV listings or best-seller lists. Ask, "Do these listings tell you everything about the shows (or books)?" What kinds of things are missing?

2. Explain that the listings give *summaries*. Write on the chalk-board:

> A summary briefly states the main ideas of an article or the main events in a story.

3. Explain that summaries of fiction and nonfiction material may differ. Note on the board:

> A summary of fictional material should briefly describe the main conflict, problem to be solved, or goal, and the other basic elements of the story (who, where, when, why and how).

> A summary of nonfictional material should tell the main ideas and important details.

4. Draw one of the herringbone diagrams shown here on the chalkboard. Ask students to help you fill out the diagram for your current Read To book. After completing the diagram, ask students to help you write a brief summary of the book.

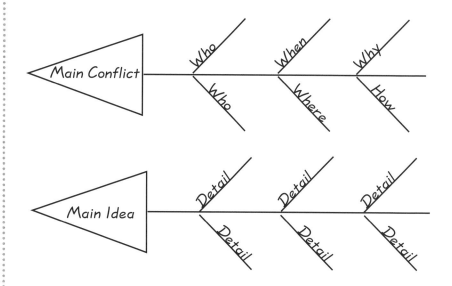

5. Remind students that the skill of summarizing has many practical uses. For example, summaries can be used as study guides, as outlines, and as closing statements in letters and compositions.

STATUS OF THE CLASS FOLLOW-UP

As you take the Status of the Class, help students summarize their books by asking questions such as:

For fiction:

- ♦ What is the main conflict (problem or goal) in the story?
- ♦ Who are the major characters in the story?
- ♦ Where and when is the story taking place?
- ♦ How is the conflict resolved?

For nonfiction:

- ♦ What is the main idea of the selection?
- ♦ What are some important details that support the main idea?

Continued on next page

ADDED PRACTICE

◆ Encourage groups of students to develop checklists for critiquing their summaries. Questions might include:
Do I understand the selection? Do I need to reread any parts?
Did I state the main idea of the selection?
Did I include only important information?
Have I conserved words? Is there a list or description that I can replace with a simple word or phrase?
Is there any information that I repeated or that I don't need?

◆ Suggest that students pretend they are the authors of their books and that they have just finished writing. Have them compose telegrams to their publishers summarizing their newly written book in thirty words or less.

◆ To emphasize the need for brevity when summarizing, have students try to read their summaries aloud in one breath.

AUTHOR'S PURPOSE

GRADE LEVEL : High School (9-12)

OBJECTIVE : To help students identify an author's purpose for writing and think critically about how an author fulfills that purpose

MATERIALS : Any book that you have read to students, such as *Animal Farm* by George Orwell (8.8)

LESSON : You may wish to teach author's purpose in two separate mini-lessons.

Day One : **1.** Ask students to brainstorm a list of the types of programs that appear on television, such as news reports, sitcoms, talk shows, dramas, and documentaries. Record students' suggestions on the chalkboard.

2. As you point to each item, ask, "Why would a television producer make this kind of show? What is the purpose?" Record students' responses and note that different programs have different purposes.

3. Select a few of the purposes recorded on the board and ask students to give examples of books or other written material that also serve each of these purposes. Ask, "Can authors have different purposes for writing, as do the producers of television programs?"

4. Hold up a Read To book, such as *Animal Farm,* and ask, "Why do you think the author wrote this book?" Students' suggestions might include:
- ◆ He wanted to give readers information about the effects of revolution.
- ◆ He wanted to tell a "what if" story about animals taking over a farm.
- ◆ He wanted to persuade readers to believe that totalitarianism is evil.

Save this list for the second day of instruction.

5. Tell students that most authors' purposes for writing fall within three main categories: to inform, to entertain, and to persuade. Go back to the list of television programs on the board and ask, "What is the primary purpose (to inform, to entertain, or to persuade) of each of these programs?"

6. Tell students that thinking about an author's purpose for writing may help them decide how to go about reading a book. Point out, for example, that a book written purely to entertain can be read fairly quickly, while a textbook, which provides information, usually requires a more careful reading.

Day Two

1. Remind students that most purposes for writing fall within three categories: to inform, to entertain, and to persuade. Ask, "Is it possible for an author to have more than one purpose for writing?" Briefly discuss examples of writing that have more than one purpose, a newspaper article, for example, that is both humorous (and therefore entertaining) and informative.

2. Hold up a current Read To book, such as *Animal Farm,* and choose one purpose, such as "to persuade readers that totalitarianism is evil." Ask, "What writing techniques does the author use to fulfill this purpose?" Students' suggestions might include:
- Word choice, as in statements such as "All animals are equal, but some animals are *more* equal than others."
- Characterization, as in stock characters like the ambitious "dictator," Napoleon, and the loyal "proletariat," Boxer.
- Plot structure, as in the decision of the animals to send Boxer to the glue factory.

3. List other literary devices, such as point of view, style, and setting, and ask how the author uses each to further his purpose in writing the book.

4. Tell students that figuring out an author's purpose and thinking about the writing techniques he uses to fulfill that purpose will help them better understand what they read.

STATUS OF THE CLASS FOLLOW-UP

As you take the Status of the Class, ask:
- ◆ Why do you think the author wrote this book?
- ◆ Does knowing the author's purpose affect how you read the book? If so, how?
- ◆ Do you think the author is fulfilling his or her purpose? What writing techniques does the author employ?

ADDED PRACTICE

- ◆ Have students create a chart like the one shown, and list authors' purposes and the techniques used to fulfill them.

Purpose	Method	Examples
To inform		
To entertain		
To persuade		

- ◆ Ask students to write three short book reviews of one book they have read, writing each review with a different purpose in mind (to inform, to entertain, or to persuade). Discuss the different writing techniques they use to fulfill each purpose.

THEME

GRADE LEVEL High School (9-12)

OBJECTIVE To help students identify the theme of a piece of writing

MATERIALS Any book that you have read to students, such as *Of Mice and Men* by John Steinbeck (8.0)

LESSON

1. Remind students that the central idea of a piece of writing is called its *theme.* Ask, "What are some ways you can figure out what a book's theme is?" As students discuss the answer, emphasize the following points:

- Finding the theme or underlying idea of a book involves considering the meaning of the text as a whole.
- A theme may be either directly or indirectly stated. A theme that is stated directly is called an *explicit* theme. A theme that is implied in characters' actions or other parts of the story is called an *implicit* theme.
- A story may have many themes, but usually there is one theme that is *primary*, or most important.

2. Hold up a Read To book, such as *Of Mice and Men,* and ask, "What is the theme of this book?" List students' responses on the board and discuss each one. Suggested themes for *Of Mice and Men* might include:

- The bonds of friendship
- The powerlessness of the laboring class
- Finding a home in a hostile world

3. Point to each suggestion and ask, "What events or actions in the book support this theme?" For example, for the theme, "The bonds of friendship," students might offer the following support:

- George and Lennie tenaciously hold onto their shared dream of owning land.
- George feels responsible for Lennie even when Lennie's actions place him in danger.
- George and Lennie understand that their friendship makes the loneliness and isolation of their lives bearable.

◆ The two men are proud of and loyal to each other.
◆ George's shooting of Lennie to protect him from the lynching is the ultimate act of love.

4. If students have trouble identifying the parts of the book that support the theme, guide their thinking by asking such questions as:
◆ What does the story seem to be all about?
◆ What is the author's point in telling this story?
◆ Does one idea come up time and time again? What is that idea?

5. Tell students that figuring out a book's theme or themes will help them think critically about what they are reading.

STATUS OF THE CLASS FOLLOW-UP

As you take the Status of the Class, ask:
◆ What is the theme of your book? If there is more than one theme, which do you think is the main theme?
◆ Which events or characters' actions support the theme?
◆ Do you know any other books that have the same theme?

ADDED PRACTICE

◆ Have students draw a Venn diagram for two books they have recently read. Have them list the major and minor themes of each book and place the common themes in the intersection of the two circles.

◆ Have students write a poem expressing the theme of a book they have recently read.

MINI-LESSON PLANNING FORM

MINI-LESSON TITLE

_____

GRADE LEVEL

_____

OBJECTIVE

_____

MATERIALS

_____

LESSON

_____

STATUS OF THE CLASS
FOLLOW-UP

_____

ADDED PRACTICE

_____